NATIVE NATIONS OF NORTH AMERICA

Nations of the

SOUTHEAST

Molly Aloian & Bobbie Kalman

Crabtree Publishing Company

www.crabtreebooks.com

Nations of the SOUTHEAST

Dedicated by Molly Aloian
For my Grandpa Sid, whose many talents and accomplishments will always be remembered.

Editor-in-Chief
Bobbie Kalman

Writing team
Molly Aloian
Bobbie Kalman

Substantive editor
Kathryn Smithyman

Editors
Robin Johnson
Kelley MacAulay

Design
Katherine Kantor

Cover design
Katherine Kantor
Samantha Crabtree

Production coordinator
Heather Fitzpatrick

Photo research
Crystal Foxton

Consultant
Dr. Charles Hudson, Honorary Director Emeritus of the Institute of Native American Studies and Professor Emeritus of Anthropology, University of Georgia

Illustrations
Barbara Bedell: page 12
Katherine Kantor: pages 4 (southeast map), 10 (skirt)
Bonna Rouse: border, pages 4 (map of North America), 14, 17, 22 (right)
Margaret Amy Salter: back cover (background), pages 5 (background), 10 (all except skirt), 22 (left), 27 (background), 29 (background), 31 (background)

Photographs and reproductions
Paintings by Martin Pate, Newnan, GA, Courtesy Southeast Archeological Center, National Park Service: front cover, pages 5, 15, 18, 23, 26
©Bryn Barnard: pages 7, 24
Courtesy of Frank H. McClung Museum, The University of Tennessee: Farmstead - Painting by Carlyle Urello: back cover, page 13 (bottom); Paleoindian - Painting by Greg Harlin: page 6
The Granger Collection, New York: pages 28, 29
Historical Artist Robert Griffing and Publisher, Paramount Press Inc.: page 27
The Oklahoma State Senate Historical Preservation Fund, Inc., Charles R. Ford, President: page 21
The Philbrook Museum of Art, Tulsa, Oklahoma: Fred Beaver (Creek-Seminole, 1911-1980), *Seminole Family at Work*, 1948, 1948.18, watercolor: page 19; Fred Beaver, *Creek Men's Feather Dance*, 1950, 1950.7, watercolor: page 8; Acee Blue Eagle (Creek-Pawnee, 1907-1959), *Creek Mother and Child*, 1946, 1946.22, watercolor: page 31; Solomon McCombs, *Creek Indian Social Ball Game*, 1857, 1957.7, watercolor: page 9 (bottom)
kRobinsonArt.com: page 30
Smithsonian American Art Museum, Washington, DC/Art Resource, NY: pages 11, 13 (top), 20
Wood Ronsaville Harlin, Inc.: ©Karen Barnes: page 9 (top); ©Matthew Frey: page 25; ©Greg Harlin: title page; ©Rob Wood: pages 16-17
Other images by Digital Vision

Crabtree Publishing Company

www.crabtreebooks.com   1-800-387-7650

Cataloging-in-Publication Data
Aloian, Molly.
Nations of the Southeast / Molly Aloian & Bobbie Kalman.
  p. cm. -- (Native nations of North America series)
Includes index.
ISBN-13: 978-0-7787-0385-3 (rlb)
ISBN-10: 0-7787-0385-1 (rlb)
ISBN-13: 978-0-7787-0477-5 (pbk)
ISBN-10: 0-7787-0477-7 (pbk)
 1. Indians of North America--Southern States--History--Juvenile literature.
2. Indians of South America--Southern States--Social life and customs--Juvenile literature. I. Kalman, Bobbie. II. Title. III. Native nations of North America.
E78.S65A654 2006
975.004'97--dc22
                                        2005022997
                                        LC

Published in the United States
PMB16A
350 Fifth Ave.
Suite 3308
New York, NY
10118

Published in Canada
616 Welland Ave.,
St. Catharines, Ontario,
Canada
L2M 5V6

Published in the United Kingdom
73 Lime Walk
Headington
Oxford
OX3 7AD
United Kingdom

Published in Australia
386 Mt. Alexander Rd.,
Ascot Vale (Melbourne)
VIC 3032

Contents

The Southeast

Indigenous, or Native, people have lived in the Southeast region of North America for at least 11,000 years. This vast region, shown on the map below, includes the present-day states of Florida, Georgia, Alabama, Mississippi, Louisiana, and South Carolina. It also includes most of present-day North Carolina, Tennessee, and Virginia, as well as parts of Texas, Oklahoma, Arkansas, Illinois, Missouri, Kentucky, West Virginia, and Maryland. The region is west of the Atlantic Ocean and north of the Gulf of Mexico.

The **climate** in the southern part of the Southeast region is warm year round. In the northern part of the region, winters are generally cool, whereas summers are usually hot and humid. The Appalachian Mountains run from the northeast down into the middle of the Southeast region. Temperatures in the mountains are cooler than are temperatures in the flatter areas. Most of the Southeast region receives plenty of rain during the warm months. Certain areas, such as lands in present-day Texas, receive little rain and are mainly dry year round.

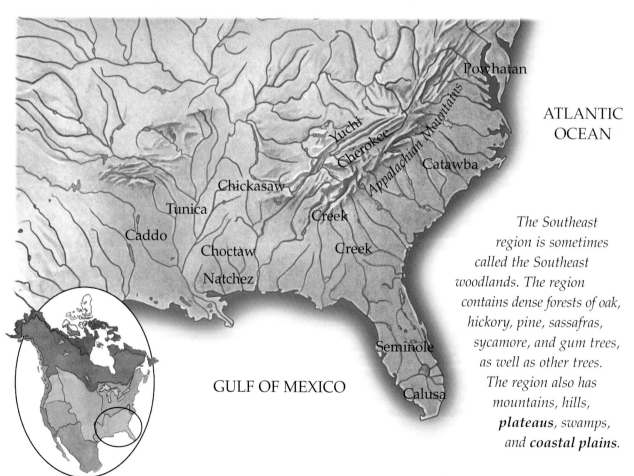

ATLANTIC OCEAN

GULF OF MEXICO

*The Southeast region is sometimes called the Southeast woodlands. The region contains dense forests of oak, hickory, pine, sassafras, sycamore, and gum trees, as well as other trees. The region also has mountains, hills, **plateaus**, swamps, and **coastal plains**.*

4

Nations and territories

This book describes some of the Native **nations** that lived in the Southeast just after the first European explorers arrived in the region in the 1500s and 1600s. Nations are groups of people with similar origins, customs, languages, and traditions. Each nation had its own **territory**, or area of land in which people fished, hunted, collected plant foods, and farmed. The approximate location of each nation's territory is shown on the map on page 4. Native people in the Southeast region lived in large permanent villages in their territories.

Forming alliances

Some of the nations in the Southeast region formed **alliances** with one another. An alliance is a friendly partnership or association between two or more nations. The nations formed alliances because they had common interests. These partnerships helped the nations achieve common goals. The alliances also helped the nations defend themselves against attacks from other nations.

Villages and towns, such as the town shown above, were often located near lakes, rivers, streams, or other waterways.

Language families

The people who lived in the Southeast spoke many languages. Each language belonged to a different **language family**. A language family is made up of languages that are similar to one another. Three of the main language families in the Southeast region were the Muskogean language family, the Siouan language family, and the Iroquoian language family. A few nations spoke different **dialects**, or versions of languages, that belonged to the same language families.

Ancient people

The first people who lived in the Southeast are called **Paleoindians** or "Old Indians." About 11,000 years ago, at the end of the **Ice Age**, the Paleoindians traveled from **Siberia** to North America. The Ice Age was a long, cold period of time during which many parts of the Earth were covered with ice. The Paleoindians were hunters. They hunted large animals such as **mammoths**. Over time, the Paleoindians and their **descendants** developed new ways of life using the **natural resources** around them.

The Archaic period

Approximately 10,000 years ago, during a period of time called the **Archaic period**, descendants of the Paleoindians began hunting deer and elk. The people did not live in one place. Instead, they moved from place to place to hunt animals. They used a hunting tool and weapon called a **javelin**. A javelin is a light, wooden spear. People also began collecting chestnuts, hickory nuts, acorns, and other wild plants for food.

Javelins and spears had stone points on their tips. These hunters are making stone points for their spears.

The Woodland period

Around 3,000 years ago, during a period of time called the **Woodland period**, people began living in permanent villages and building **burial mounds** in their villages. Burial mounds were mounds of earth that were built to honor dead village members. At about this time, people began growing seed-bearing plants, such as sunflowers, marsh elder, and squash. They also made bowls and pots out of **fired clay**.

Mississippian period

Around 1,000 years ago, during a period of time called the **Mississippian period**, people began growing corn and beans. Corn and beans fed more people than seed-bearing plants did. As a result, villages grew in size. The people in the villages organized themselves into **chiefdoms**, or large groups led by powerful chiefs.

The people who lived during the Mississippian period built large earth mounds in their villages.

Burial and temple mounds

People built burial mounds to show respect for village members who had died. To build burial mounds, people worked together piling earth on and around the graves of honored members of their villages. Many burial mounds were between 30 and 40 feet (9-12 m) high. In addition to building burial mounds, people built **temple mounds** in their villages.

Temple mounds were mounds upon which **temples** were built. Temples are buildings in which people hold religious ceremonies. The picture above shows a Mississippian village called Moundville, which existed in present-day Alabama. The home of the village ruler stands at the top of the mound. Although the Mississippians stopped building mounds in about 1550, some mounds still exist today. The mounds have been rebuilt and **preserved**, or saved.

The Creek Confederacy

When English traders arrived in present-day Georgia in the late 1600s, they encountered thousands of Native people living along a stream. The English called the stream "Ochesee Creek" and began calling all the Native people in the area "Ochesee Creeks." Eventually, the English shortened this name to "Creeks."

Native towns

The people known as the "Creeks" were not all part of the same nation—several nations lived in the area. The people of these nations lived in separate villages and spoke different languages. Each village had a different Native name and had its own chiefs. The nations had a loose alliance with one another, however. They formed this alliance when they needed to protect themselves from being attacked by some of the nations that lived north of the region. More than twelve nations became part of the alliance.

Growing colonies

In the 1700s, Europeans created **colonies** in the region. The colonies spread into more and more Native territories. The nations strengthened their alliance to protect their territories from **colonists**, and later, from Americans. The colonists and Americans called the alliance the "Creek **Confederacy**." A confederacy is a group of nations that join together and have equal power.

These Creek men are participating in a ceremonial dance called the Feather Dance.

The Muskogee

Most of the Creeks spoke languages that belonged to the Muskogean language family. As a result, the Creeks are often referred to as "the Muskogee." The Muskogee were one nation in the area. The Muskogee and the other nations in the Creek Confederacy were descendants of the Mississippian people. For many years, the Muskogee lived in a territory in present-day Alabama and Georgia. More than 50 of their villages were located along the banks of creeks and rivers. Between 100 and 1,000 people lived in each Muskogee village.

(above) All the people in a Muskogee town worked hard to ensure that there was enough food for everyone. Young girls learned how to grow and prepare various foods by watching their mothers.

(left) Many of the nations in the Creek Confederacy played ball games during the summer months. Both men and women enjoyed playing these games.

Natchez, Tunica, and Caddo

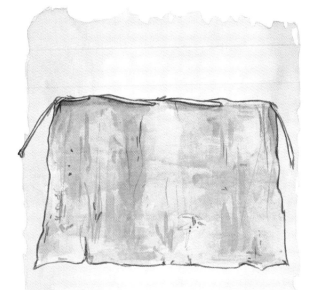

Natchez women made clothing, including the skirt shown above, by pounding the inner bark of mulberry trees. They also used plant materials to make baskets and fishing nets.

The Tunica collected water from saltwater springs and then heated the water until the salt could be removed. They used salt to add flavor to foods. They also traded salt to other nations.

The Natchez, the Tunica, and the Caddo lived in territories in the western part of the Southeast region. These three nations were made up of thousands of people.

The Natchez

The Natchez were one of the largest and most powerful nations in the Southeast region. The nation had between 4,000 and 4,500 members, who lived in more than nine villages. Their territory was along the banks of the lower Mississippi River in present-day Mississippi. The ways of life of the Natchez were similar to the ways of life of the people who lived during the Mississippian period. The Natchez preserved the Mississippian ways of life longer than their neighboring nations did.

The Tunica

The Tunica nation lived in the northwestern part of present-day Mississippi and in the eastern parts of present-day Arkansas and Louisiana. Many Tunica villages were located near the Mississippi River on the Mississippi **flood plain**. A flood plain is an area around a river that floods often. Flooding produces **fertile** soil. Fertile soil is rich in nutrients. It is good for growing corn, beans, squash and other crops. In the late 1600s, about 2,000 Tunica people lived in these areas. They spoke a language that was also called "Tunica." The language belonged to the Tunican language family.

The Caddo

The Caddo people called themselves "Kadohadacho" or "real chiefs." They were part of a confederacy called "the Caddo Confederacy." In the 1600s, there may have been as many as twelve nations in the Caddo Confederacy, including the Natchitoches nation, the Adai nation, and the Yatasi nation. The Caddo were the most powerful nation in the confederacy, however.

All the nations in the Caddo confederacy had territories on both sides of the Red River, in present-day Louisiana, Arkansas, Oklahoma, and Texas. In the early 1600s, about 10,000 people lived in these areas. The language they spoke was also "Caddo." It belonged to the Caddoan language family. Some historians believe that the Caddo once lived in the Southwest and traveled across the **prairies** to their territory in the Southeast region.

Herds of buffalo sometimes roamed the prairies west of Caddo territory. In the late 1600s, some Caddo hunters acquired horses from European traders. The hunters chased the buffalo on the horses. When the hunters got close enough, they shot the buffalo with bows and arrows.

Chickasaw, Choctaw, and Cherokee

The Chickasaw, the Choctaw, and the Cherokee are three nations that lived in the Southeast region. The Chickasaw and the Choctaw spoke closely related languages and had similar cultures. Both nations spoke languages from the Muskogean language family. People from the Cherokee nation spoke a language that belonged to the Iroquoian language family.

The Chickasaw

In the 1500s, there were about 15,000 members of the Chickasaw nation. Chickasaw territory was located in the northern part of present-day Mississippi and in the Mississippi Valley. The territory also stretched east into present-day Tennessee, Kentucky, and Alabama. Along the Mississippi River, Chickasaw territory was located on a flood plain, so the soil was ideal for growing crops. The people who lived on the flood plain built their villages on areas of high ground, so their homes would not be flooded when the banks of the Mississippi River overflowed.

*Like most warriors, Chickasaw warriors painted their faces to show their personalities and to **intimidate**, or frighten, their enemies.*

The Choctaw

The Choctaw are descendants of the people who lived during the Mississippian period. The Choctaw lived in the southern part of present-day Mississippi and in the western part of present-day Alabama. They also had territory in the eastern part of present-day Louisiana. In the mid 1500s, there may have been between 15,000 and 20,000 members of the Choctaw nation.

Choctaw women planted and grew crops, prepared food, and made clothing. They decorated some of the clothes with colorful animal or human figures. They used plant dyes to make the colors.

The Cherokee

The Cherokee called themselves "Ani-yun-wiya," which meant "real people" in their language. In the mid 1500s, there were about 29,000 members of the Cherokee nation living in as many as 100 villages. Large villages were often located near waterways. Cherokee territory was in the Appalachian **highlands**, or mountainous sections of land. It spanned several present-day states, including North Carolina, Kentucky, Tennessee, Virginia, South Carolina, Georgia, and Alabama. The territory was extremely large, so historians often divide it into lower, middle, and upper sections. The people in each section spoke different dialects of the Cherokee language.

Powhatan and Yuchi

The Powhatan and the Yuchi are two nations that had similar ways of life. They lived in different territories and spoke different languages, however.

The Powhatan

Powhatan territory was in present-day Virginia, in an area of land known today as the Tidewater region. The people called their territory "Tsenacommacah," which meant "densely inhabited land" in their language. The region included many thick forests. It also included several rivers, which all flowed into Chesapeake Bay. The people hunted in the forests and fished in the rivers. The Powhatan language belonged to the Algonquian language family. The Powhatan nation was part of a confederacy, called the Powhatan Confederacy, with about six other nations, including the Mattaponi and the Pamunkey nations. Over time, more and more nations joined the confederacy. By 1607, over 30 nations were part of the confederacy. A powerful leader named Wahunsonacock ruled all the nations as a chiefdom.

Both the Powhatan, shown above, and the Yuchi lived in villages that were surrounded by small vegetable gardens and large fields of crops.

The Yuchi

In the mid 1500s, the Yuchi people may have lived in eastern Tennessee. By the late 1600s, they moved to the area of land around the Savannah River and into parts of present-day South Carolina, Georgia, and Florida. There were at least 2,500 members of the Yuchi nation in the mid 1600s. The nation was made up of several **bands**, or groups, of people. Each band had its own Native name. The people of the Yuchi nation spoke a language called "Yuchean." It was not related to any other languages spoken in the Southeast region.

Like most villages in the Southeast region, Yuchi villages included homes that were grouped around **plazas**. *A plaza is a public square or open area in a town or village. People played games and held ceremonies and other social events in the plazas.*

Calusa and Catawba

The Calusa and the Catawba were both large nations. In the early 1500s, the Calusa nation may have had more than 50,000 members. There may have been more than 10,000 members of the Catawba nation.

The Calusa

The Calusa had territory in the southwestern part of present-day Florida. The climate in this area is **subtropical**. Soil in subtropical areas is often not good for farming, so the Calusa did not grow crops. Instead, they caught fish, lobsters, and crabs from the ocean and the other waterways near their territory. They also gathered foods, such as clams and oysters, from the ocean, as shown left. They used clam and oyster shells to make bowls, utensils, jewelry, and other items.

The Catawba

The Catawba nation lived in a territory located throughout the present-day states of North Carolina and South Carolina. The Catawba River runs through this area, and many villages were located along it. Some of the Catawba people were known as "Issas" or "Esaws," which means "People of the river." Like the other nations that lived in the Southeast, the Catawba were farmers. They grew crops of corn, beans, and squash. They also hunted animals in the forests and caught fish in the rivers within their territory.

Women of the Catawba nation dug up clay from pits along the Catawba River. They formed the clay into sturdy cooking pots and decorative ceremonial pots, such as the one shown right.

Seminole

During the 1700s, colonists in the present-day states of Alabama and Georgia were fighting over Native lands. In order to escape the fighting, the Native people in the area moved south to the present-day state of Florida. Many of the nations that did not flee were later forced out of their territories by the colonists. Although most of the Native people who moved were from the Muskogee nation, people from other nations, including the Oconee and the Yamasee, were also forced to move.

One name

Even though people from several nations had moved south, the colonists did not acknowledge the differences between them. They began calling all the Native people in the area "Seminole." The name "Seminole" comes from the Spanish word "cimarron," which means "wild" or "runaway." The Native people in Florida were soon joined by black slaves who had escaped from **plantations** in the nearby colonies. The escaped slaves hoped to live and raise their families peacefully in the South. The Native people welcomed the slaves into their villages. They often hid the slaves from the colonists, who wanted to take them back to the plantations. Over time, some of the Native people and the black people **intermarried**.

Seminole territory was located near the Atlantic Ocean and the Gulf of Mexico. The people caught fish and gathered shellfish from both bodies of water.

The Everglades

The Seminole lived in the northern part of present-day Florida during the early 1700s. Before long, the colonists wanted to claim this land for themselves, as well. They forced the Seminole to move farther south, into swampy areas of land. These swampy areas are known today as the "Everglades."

In the early 1800s, there were about 1,500 members of the Seminole nation in the area. During the next 20 years, more slaves moved to the area. The Native people and the slaves continued to intermarry, and their families became larger and larger. Over time, the nation grew to about 5,000 members.

*Although living in the Everglades was difficult, the Seminole learned how to find food in the area. They also learned how to use the natural resources around them to make homes. The Seminole built homes called **chickees**, shown above. To keep their homes out of mud and water, they built the homes about three feet above the ground. They left the walls open to let air flow through.*

Towns, clans, and social classes

Some of the nations in the Southeast region divided their towns into **red towns** and **white towns**. Red towns were war towns. During times of war, a nation's warriors gathered together, held war ceremonies, and planned for war in red towns. Warriors from red towns defended all the nation's towns from attacks. White towns were peace towns. **Councils**, or meetings to settle disagreements and to establish peace between the nations, took place in white towns. People from nations that had been defeated or captured during wars often lived in peace towns.

The people in each town belonged to **clans**. Clans are groups of people who share the same **ancestors**. Some clans were named after animals, such as deer or birds. Other clans were named after elements of nature, such as the wind. In the Southeast region, clans were **matrilineal**. In matrilineal clans, a child became part of his or her mother's clan as soon as the child was born. The members of a clan thought of one another as family, even though we would think of them as being only distantly related to one another.

People from different towns and clans played games of stickball for fun and to settle disagreements with one another. Hundreds of people played on large fields that were up to 900 feet (274 m) long.

Social classes

The people of some nations, including the Natchez and the Caddo, were divided into two **classes**, or ranks of people. One class was made up of chiefs and their relatives. The other class was made up of **commoners**. Commoners were people who farmed, built homes, provided the chiefs and their relatives with food and gifts, and performed other physical tasks. The chiefs of nations that had two classes could not marry other chiefs. The chiefs had to marry commoners. This class system is believed to be a tradition that began during the Mississippian period.

Chiefs

Each town had one or more chiefs. Some towns had red chiefs, who were war chiefs, and white chiefs, who were peace chiefs. War chiefs ruled during times of war, whereas peace chiefs ruled during times of peace. The people of some nations called their chiefs "mikos." Many towns also had clan leaders, who had authority over all the members of a clan. Some towns and clans had female chiefs, whereas others had male chiefs. Men and women usually inherited their roles as chiefs from their clans. Other chiefs were chosen based on their **merits**, or their abilities and achievements.

Overseers and leaders

Chiefs oversaw the activities that took place in towns or within clans. They also acted as leaders during councils. Some chiefs were advisors, but they had little power over the actions of people. Other chiefs had great power over their people.

*Town chiefs and clan chiefs attended councils. **Elders**, or older, respected members of towns and villages, also attended councils and helped make decisions.*

Village life

Villages in the Southeast region were made up of groups of houses, which were built around open plazas. Most villages contained many houses, but some villages were made up of only a few houses. The people of some nations built **palisades** around their villages. Palisades are walls made from wooden poles that are sharpened to points at their tops. The palisades protected villagers from attacks during times of war.

Different houses
Native people made their homes from natural materials such as wood, animal skins, clay, bark, and **thatch**. Different nations built different homes. The Cherokee built **wattle-and-daub** homes. The people of some nations, such as the Caddo, built houses made of grass, as shown above. Many nations also built storage houses that were used to keep food and other items out of the wind, rain, and heat, and away from hungry animals.

Growing crops
Farming was an important part of village life. Most villages were surrounded by fertile land that was ideal for growing crops of corn, squash, sunflowers, pumpkins, beans, and tobacco. Men created fields for crops by **clearing** areas of land. To clear land, they set small fires that burned away trees, shrubs, and grass in the areas near their villages. Women were usually responsible for planting the seeds and collecting the crops.

Green Corn Ceremony

In late summer of every year, most nations in the Southeast region held a ceremony called the Green Corn Ceremony. The ceremony was an important part of village life and marked the beginning of the new year. People celebrated the ripe corn crops and offered thanks for all they had received from the land throughout the year. In each village, people put out all their household fires and lit just one fire, called the **sacred fire**, in the ceremonial area of their village. The household fires were then relit from the sacred fire. People danced, sang songs, told stories, and **fasted**, or went without food. The fasting was followed by large feasts. The Green Corn Ceremony often lasted several days.

Finding food

Although many of the Native people in the Southeast region were farmers, they still hunted, fished, and gathered plant foods in their territories. They lived in permanent villages, but at certain times of the year, people from each village traveled to fishing, hunting, and gathering spots within their territories and set up temporary camps. Men were skilled hunters and fishers, and women knew when and where to gather plant foods. Men fished in the waterways that surrounded their villages and caught animals in the forests. Women searched the forests for wild plant foods and knew which foods were safe to eat. Native people never killed more animals or gathered more foods than they needed, however. They were always thankful to the animals for giving up their lives to feed people.

*To kill birds and other small animals, hunters sometimes shot wooden darts out of **blow guns**, such as the one shown left. The blow guns were made from hollow cane stems, which were up to 10 feet (3 m) long.*

Hunting

Hunters knew where to find the animals they needed in order to survive. The animals provided Native families with meat and other important materials, such as bones, furs, and **hides**, or animal skins. Men hunted many animals, including buffalo, deer, bears, turkeys, and rabbits. Some hunters used traps to catch animals. Others shot animals with bows and arrows. Some hunters got close to deer by covering themselves in deerskins, with the heads and antlers still attached. The hunters moved around like deer. When the deer approached, the hunters shot the animals with bows and arrows.

Fishing

Some people fished from canoes, whereas others fished from the banks of rivers, lakes, or streams. Many fishers used hooks and lines to catch fish. Others fished using spears, traps, nets, and bows and arrows. Chickasaw fishers caught huge catfish in the Mississippi River. These fish sometimes weighed up to 200 pounds (91 kg)! Women preserved the fish and meat to prevent these foods from spoiling. They dried them in the sun or smoked them over fires.

Gathering

Women and girls gathered roots, seeds, nuts, fruits, mushrooms, as well as herbs and bird eggs. They also gathered various plants to use as medicines. The women of some nations, including the Chickasaw and the Choctaw, gathered sassafras roots and made hot tea from the roots.

This man is using a net to catch birds. The net is made from plant materials. The woman beside him is gathering bird eggs.

Trading goods

Trade was an important part of life for many Southeast nations. People traveled on foot or by canoe in order to trade items with people from other nations. Trade routes included lakes, rivers, and paths through forests. Traders traveled the same trade routes several times each year.

Long-distance trade

The people of many Southeast nations traded items with other nations in the Southeast region. They also traded with people that lived outside the region.

For example, the Tunica and the Caddo exchanged goods with the Quapaw nation, who lived in a territory west of the Southeast region. The Chickasaw may have occasionally traded with people from as far away as the present-day country of Mexico! Both men and women prepared goods for trade, but men usually traveled from place to place to exchange the goods. Whether they lived in nearby territories or far away from one another, traders treated one another with respect. They made sure that the trades were fair for everyone involved.

Women of some nations made fired clay pots, bowls, and other containers, which were traded for different goods that were wanted or needed.

Goods for trade

Items acquired during hunting trips, such as animal skins and furs, were commonly traded for handmade items, including pipes, bowls, and spoons. People from the Cherokee and Natchez nations made pipes that were greatly admired throughout the Southeast region. The nations also traded items that were abundant in their territories for items that were not available to them. For example, the people of some nations, such as the Tunica and the Caddo, collected salt from mines and salt springs. They then traded the salt to nations throughout the Southeast that did not have salt in their territories. Many nations traded items for **yaupon** leaves. Yaupon is a type of holly that grew near the coasts of the Atlantic Ocean and the Gulf of Mexico. Native people used the leaves to make tea. They drank the tea daily to cleanse their bodies and minds. They also drank it before councils, Green Corn Ceremonies, and other important events.

Trading with Europeans

The people of most Native nations also traded goods with European traders and colonists. By the early 1700s, most Native nations traded animal furs and skins for European goods such as copper kettles, metal knives, guns, cloth, and alcohol, such as rum. Over time, Native people used more and more of these goods. They began using non-Native goods instead of their traditional tools and weapons. As a result, their ways of life began to change.

Many Native people, including people from the Cherokee nation, shown right, acquired guns and cloth from European traders.

A changing world

This painting shows people of the Caddo nation meeting to trade with Europeans.

Alcohol and diseases

Some Europeans traded alcohol to Native people in exchange for animal skins and furs. Native people had never before tasted alcohol and did not know its effects. As a result, some Native people became addicted to alcohol. Some Europeans intentionally traded alcohol to get Native people to agree to unfair or unequal trades. Europeans also brought diseases such as smallpox and typhus into Native villages, which the Native people had never before encountered. Native people did not have any natural defenses against these diseases. Shortly after coming into contact with Europeans and European goods, thousands of Native people became sick and died.

The presence of European explorers, traders, and colonists had devastating effects on the lives of Native people. As Native people and Europeans continued to trade, Europeans began demanding more and more furs and skins from Native traders. In order to satisfy the Europeans, Native people began hunting too many deer and other animals. The men spent more and more time on hunting trips, away from their families and villages. They hunted more animals than they needed, and certain animal populations began to decrease. As a result, many Native families were no longer able to continue practicing their traditional ways of life.

Losing their territories

During the 1600s, Spanish **missionaries** built **missions**, or churches, along the coasts of the Atlantic Ocean and the Gulf of Mexico. The missionaries often forced the Native people to give up their traditional spiritual beliefs and convert to Christianity. During this time, new colonies were expanding into Native territories. During the 1700s, the French and the English fought several wars over Native lands in the Southeast. Some of the nations in the region fought one another for territories, as well. Native people struggled to protect their lands, but many towns and villages were destroyed. By 1750, the populations of many nations had greatly declined due to wars and **epidemics**. The survivors from several nations joined together.

The Trail of Tears

In the early 1800s, after the **American Revolution**, American people did not want Native people living on the lands they had claimed as their own. The American people pressured the United States government to remove the Native people from the new states in the Southeast. In 1830, the government passed the Indian Removal Act, which forced Native people to move. Between 1830 and 1840, about 60,000 Native people were forced to leave their homes and many of their possessions and move to **Indian Territory**.

Indian Territory was an area of land west of the Mississippi River that was set aside for Native people. For thousands of people, the journey to Indian Territory was over 1,000 miles (1609 km) long. Many Native people died from starvation and exhaustion along the way. Today, the journey is known as "The Trail of Tears." Originally, this phrase referred to the removal of the Cherokee nation. The phrase now refers to the removal of the Cherokee, Creek, Chickasaw, Choctaw, and Seminole nations. All of these nations were sent to Indian Territory during the 1800s.

Becoming "civilized"

After they arrived in Indian Territory, Native people felt even more pressure from Americans to change their ways of life. Americans tried to "civilize" the Native people by encouraging them to give up their languages, traditions, and Native beliefs. Eventually, many people from the Cherokee, Chickasaw, Choctaw, Creek, and Seminole nations dressed like Americans, practiced Christianity, adopted American styles of government, and used American farming methods such as raising **livestock**, or farm animals. The people of these nations also established businesses and created public school systems. Americans called these nations the "Five Civilized Tribes" because the Native people quickly adopted many American ways of life.

The nations today

Despite the hardships they have endured, Native people continue to live throughout much of North America. Today, hundreds of thousands of people from the Creek, Cherokee, Seminole, Chickasaw, and Choctaw nations, as well as people from several other nations, live in the Southeast region and throughout North America. Many Native people work hard to preserve their languages, cultures, traditions, and sacred places. They also make pots and baskets in the traditional ways. Many participate in some of the same ceremonies that were once practiced by their ancestors. By honoring the traditions of their ancestors, they help keep their cultures alive. Several nations, including the Cherokee, the Caddo, and the Catawba, are recognized by the federal government. When a nation is recognized by the federal government, the people of that nation are eligible to receive benefits from the government.

The picture above is called Seminole Moons. It was painted by Karen Robinson, an artist who has Cherokee ancestors.

Sharing the past

In the past, many Native people did not have the same opportunities as non-Native people had. Today, Native people hold a wide variety of jobs in both Native communities and non-Native communities. Many Native people still speak their Native languages and make it a priority to teach younger generations the histories of their nations. Teaching younger generations helps ensure that people will continue to learn about the past and present Native nations in the Southeast region and throughout North America.

Proud of their heritages

Today, many Native people live on **reservations**. A reservation is a specific area of land that has been set aside by the government for Native people. Each reservation has its own government, so members can create their own laws. Many nations continue to be governed by councils that meet to discuss important issues. Few Southeastern Native people live near the territories in which their ancestors once lived. No matter where they live, however, Native people are proud of their cultures and strive to keep their traditions alive.

Glossary

Note: Boldfaced words that are defined in the book may not appear in the glossary.

American Revolution The war between the American colonies and Great Britain (1775-1783), which led to the formation of the United States

ancestor A person, usually farther back in a family's history than grandparents, from whom someone is descended

climate The long-term weather conditions in an area, including temperature, rainfall, and wind

coastal plain Flat land that is near the ocean

colonist A person who lives in a colony

colony An area of land that is ruled by a faraway country and is occupied by settlers from that faraway country

descendant A person who comes from a particular ancestor or group of ancestors

epidemic An outbreak of a disease that spreads quickly

fired clay Clay that has been dried by heating it in a fire or in the sun

intermarry To marry a person who is a member of another group

mammoth A large, hairy species of elephant that no longer lives on Earth

missionary A priest or other religious person who tries to convert others to his or her religion

natural resources Useful materials that are available in nature

plantation A large farm on which crops such as tobacco, cotton, or sugar are raised

plateau An elevated area of flat land

prairie A large area of flat, treeless land in the central part of North America

Siberia A region in the central and eastern parts of Russia

subtropical Describing areas of land and water that are close to the tropics, which is a hot region located near the equator

thatch Straw, grass, or other plant materials that are used to cover roofs

wattle-and-daub Grass or twigs that are interwoven and plastered together with mud or clay

Index

1 2 3 4 5 6 7 8 9 0   Printed in the U.S.A.   4 3 2 1 0 9 8 7 6 5